Alter Mundus

Lucia Gazzino

Alter Mundus

Translated by

Michael Daley

Pleasure Boat Studio: A Literary Press
New York

First Published in 2004 in Italy by Lietocolle Press

Poetry
ISBN 978-1-929355-94-5
Library of Congress Control Number: 2013904873

Cover art: "Alter Mundus," oil on canvas,
by Massimo Malipiero

Book and Cover Design by Tonya Namura
using Minion Pro

Published by Pleasure Boat Studio: A Literary Press
www.pleasureboatstudio.com

Table of Contents

Preface

This collection of poems knows no surrender because it is a portrait of dignity and of declaratory urgency. It is a state of wonder that knows pain and grief because it evokes deep life-paths and transforms the duration of being with the colors of the extreme gift of love. The poetry of Gazzino is lucid awareness, inclined to sacrifice for truth, for the purity of human contact and the common conscience.

Alter Mundus is an organic diary of reflections that become reality in the full maturity of emancipation, in remembrance, in the amorous instinct. These are refined lyrics, extremely personal, with a sweet timbre—the lyrical mark of a great identity, even when it explores the contradictions and the assertions of the Id.

This collection sinks its own roots in the soul of the most intimate sensations and, at times, the poems are amulets against the inhumanity of the world, and the anxieties are the unity and celebration of love. But beware: there is no guilt or submission in not wanting to change one's destiny, but rather a humble expression of moral greatness and respect for all passages of life, even the painful ones.

Even in her 'civil' lyrics Gazzino never sits in judgment, but instead is a passionate rebel against the injustices of society, always devoted to the speech of the unfortunate and the excluded.

In reading this collection one develops the feeling that every poem is a path to knowledge, a proper rejection of the volatile compass of everyday frivolity and a firm mooring for the indomitable passions of the heart.

Ivano Malcotti | Translated by Alipio Terenzi

Introduction

This book is a particular joy for me to write an introduction to, not only because it will hopefully help present Lucia Gazzino to an American audience; but I am joined by two other admirers of her work: the noted poet and translator from the Northwest of the United States, Michael Daley, who has done a terrific job in bringing the many lyrical nuances of Lucia's poems to light, and one of the most socially and politically engaged younger poets of Italy, Ivano Malcotti (I recall translating his brilliant homage to the Haitian-American painter Jean-Michel Basquiat a few years ago), who has contributed the Preface.

I first read *Alter Mundus* when it appeared a few years ago and had been struck by the exquisite intimacy of many of her poems of love and despair as well as by the strength and resoluteness of her "civil" or more directly political poems. I wasn't wrong to send the book to Michael Daley, a fellow poet I've known since the '80s who, after a reading I gave in Seattle which he attended, expressed the desire to translate a book from Italian. Mike is likewise a poet of intimate nuance and social awareness and the result here is a translation that captures Gazzino's bitten-lip idiom, her implosive magmatic tension between "being here" and "being away."

In fact Gazzino's work is not altogether unknown in the United States, though she made her debut as a translator a few years ago when CC.Marimbo Books of Berkeley, headed by the ever-engaged poet-publisher Randy Fingland, published Lucia's translations of poems written originally in the Friulan language—a distinct langauge spoken and read mostly as a second language in the north-east zone of Italy—by the great poet and filmmaker Pier Paolo Pasolini, under the title *The New Youth*.

Like Pasolini, Gazzino writes in both Italian and Friulan, and can also write in English. Most everyone in

Italy who talks poetry talks of Pasolini. To read Pasolini's Friulan poems is to read him in his most directly simple tone and imagery. And though Lucia's Friulan is from Udine and Pasolini from Casarsa, that linguistic dimension certainly plays a part in infusing her Italian writing. I especially get that sense of simplicity and directness of tone in one of her many superb love poems, "Looking for Goodbye," where the repetitions are clearly a power from a linguistic "other world."

The *Alter Mundus*, or *Other World* that is the title of the book and the title of its most brilliant political poem is not, I'm suggesting, just a social reference but is also a linguistic one, that it's the invisible Friulan dimension that speaks through Gazzino's Italian and which Michael Daley has so sensitively if unconsciously captured in his translations.

This is a book in which despairs are never without hope and surfaces never do not go in the direction of the wisdom of woman in facing the pain of love or loss, and in affirming the nourishing self through those very confrontations in quest of revealing the clearing where truth and beauty lie, and where

For all those times
you can't return
I put my face
on your reflection
in the pane of time.

—Jack Hirschman

L’altro mondo

L’altro mondo
quello che non vuoi vedere
deturpa il tuo senso estetico
rende insonni le tue notti
umilia la tua ricchezza
E’ sporco, immondo, malato
e non cela la tua corruzione.

Dai niños de rua del Sud America
ai figli del Tibet malati di TBC
dalla donna stuprata
per un permesso di soggiorno
al bambino usato, violato
in pellicole per pseudo adulti
dalla prostituta in cerca d’amore
agli uomini della notte
persi nei loro cartoni
ai pazzi immersi nelle loro sfere,
questo è l’altro mondo!

Riscatta la tua disattenzione
mortifica la tua pigrizia

The Other World

The other world
you don't want to see
scars your sense of the aesthetic,
keeps you wide awake through the night,
disparages your treasures.
It is filth, foul, sick,
and can't hide your depravity.

From homies of South America
to boys of Tibet sick with TB,
from the woman whose rape
is the price of a place to sleep
to the child, worn out, violated
in films for so-called adults,
from the whore in search of love
to the men of the night
wasted on their cardboard,
to lunatics immersed in spheres of hell:
this is the other world!

It redeems your carelessness,
puts to shame your indolence,

tormenta il cuscino morbido
su cui posi i neuroni a riposare

E' lì per te quest'alter mundus
per rendere le lacrime,
sul tuo caviale scaduto,
ancora più fasulle
come l'opulenza di cui sei fatto

E' qui per me che non
ho altr'arma se non
l'inchiostro e fogli da sprecare
è qui per le mie amnesie momentanee
in cui rifuggo il mondo, questo o l'altro.
Sono qui perché
sono tutto e niente
e di entrambi i mondi sono figlia.

pounds the pillow smooth
where you give your brains a rest.

It exists, this *alter mundus,*
for you, above your rotten caviar,
shedding tears
almost as fake
as the opulence of your birth.

It is here for me, unarmed except
for inkwell and paper I squander,
to cure my temporary amnesia,
where I flee the world, this one or the other.
I am here because
I am everything and nothing
and I am daughter of both worlds.

Testamento

Non posso lasciarti i miei occhi
occhi che ti amarono tanto
né queste mani che sfiorarono la tua pelle
né le mie labbra che conobbero
il dolce liquore delle tue parole.
Non posso lasciarti il mio cuore
né i miei capelli o le gote o i lobi
né vesti o gioielli
Ti lascio un luogo, un vento del Nord
un mare infinito, un profumo
notturno.
Ti lascio solo il ricordo di me

Testament

I cannot leave you my eyes,
eyes that find so much love in you,
neither these hands that would caress your skin
nor my lips that would drink in
the sweet liqueur of your words.
I cannot leave you my heart
nor my hair, cheeks, earlobes,
no gowns or jewels.
I leave you a place, a wind out of the North,
a sea, infinite, a perfume,
nocturnal.
I leave you only this trace of me.

Fuso del tempo

Mi manchi già
mentre piange il cuore,
mentre gli occhi già
avvolti di nebbia
non riconoscono
questi segni.
mi manchi già
nei giorni futuri
che oltrepasseranno le paure
e la mia anima si avvolge
come seta attorno
al fuso del tempo

Spindle of Time

I miss you already
while tears well in the heart,
while eyes already
wrapped in fog
fail to recognize
these signs.
I already miss you
in the days to come
that shall overcome the terrors,
and my spirit twirls itself
like silk attuned
to the spindle of time.

Superfluo

Andarmene da qui
da questo brandello
di realtà. Realtà cieca:
non vede il necessario
e ti concede solo il superfluo

Superfluous

To depart from here
from this shredded rag
of reality. Reality, blind,
does not see the necessary,
permits only the superfluous.

Day Hospital

Oncologia Udine—1999 dicembre

C'è un albero di Natale
e lustrini e luci rosse
e pacchi colorati,
... proprio come a casa

Ci sono quadri vivaci
alle pareti e una musica caraibica
... proprio come a casa

Ci sono camici verdi
e risate laggiù nella sala
e il sorriso contagioso
di un infermiere che accenna
a un passo di tango
... a casa non ballo il tango

Siamo seduti qui in attesa
dell'ultima chemio dell'anno
noi, che li portiamo
e loro, che se ne stanno andando via

Nelle loro vene una flebo
nella nostra mente

Day Hospital, Oncology

Udine—December 1999

There is a tree for Christmas
and tinsel and lights, florid,
and tinted refreshments
...just like at home.

There are vivacious paintings
along the walls, and music of the Caribbean
...just like home.

There are surgical gowns, green,
and laughter echoing down the hall,
and the contagious smile
of an orderly hints at
a tango step—
...at home I don't tango.

We are seated here awaiting
the year's final chemo,
we, who carry them
and they who are going away.

In their veins an I-V drip,
in our minds

una lastra nera e una macchia bianca
... non è proprio come a casa

Sulle poltrone mentre
sgoccia il farmaco lento
un chiacchiericcio continuo
sui figli, mariti, mogli
e l'ultima conquista,
la classifica dell'infermiera più carina
e del medico più stronzo
Una gara sul numero dei cicli
e sul vomito post farmaco
sulle vene indurite
e un banco scommesse silenziose
su quel compagno che non si vede più.

Ma la speranza
che ci accompagna vedendoli così,
si corrode su una pagina di giornale
a cui non riesci a dare più un senso
e piangi senza lacrime
... proprio come a casa

a black slab and a white stain
…it's not exactly like home.

In the armchairs while
the meds trickle slowly,
gossip continues
about children, husbands, wives,
and the latest winnings,
the ratings held by the nurse, the prettier one,
and by the doctor, who's an asshole.
A contest over the number of cycles
before nausea induced by meds
into worn-out veins,
and a silent betting pool
over which old friend they'll see no more.

But the hope
that accompanies us witnessing them
corrodes on a page of the news
where we find even less meaning
and you weep without tears
…just like at home.

Le barriere della mente

Sono le barriere della mente
che storpiano i nostri giorni
si incuneano in noi false
disperazioni per una unghia spezzata,
per una fila saltata
per una ruga in più.
Si trasformano poi i mesi
in mete deluse e
ciechi si fanno i sensi
e gli occhi non vedono
il vero ma solo
realtà predigerite
perfette, false e striscianti

The Barriers of the Mind

They are the barriers of the mind
that cripple our days.
They wedge themselves in our false
desperations over a broken fingernail,
over our place jumped in the waiting line,
or over one more wrinkle.
Months transform themselves
into unachievable goals;
so impaired do they make the senses,
the eyes don't see
truth but a reality predigested,
perfected, false and slimy.

Il mondo è malato

Il mondo è malato
di lucida follia:
col bisturi recide
l'imperfezione minuscola
senza significato
e lascia intatto il bubbone
di deviazione perversa

Il mondo è malato
di superficialità oleosa
di viscido commercio
e con bilancia starata
pesa la carne umana
che vale meno di niente.

Il mondo è malato
di criminale e potente
vanità in cui supremi
regnano burattini
alimentati dal loro
stesso escremento mentale

Il mondo è malato
non c'è pozione

The World's Diseased

The world's diseased
with slick insanity:
scalpels excise
miniscule—meaningless—
imperfection,
and leave untouched
the perverse tumor.

The world's diseased
from greasy superficiality,
from commercial slime,
and with unbalanced scales
measures human meat
priced beneath despair.

The world's diseased
by criminal and powerful
vanity with which supreme
reigning puppets
feed on their own
excrement of mind.

The world's diseased
without a potion
to cure it;

che possa curarlo
solo le salate lacrime
di chi lo ama ancora
salgono al cielo
e mutano gli orrori
in pioggia che
lava, disseta e sfama.

only the salt tears
of one who still loves it
sail to the clouds
and change the horror
into rain
to cleanse, quench, and feed.

In cerca di un addio

Per tutte le volte
che non riuscivi a dire
“ti amo”
l’ho detto io per te
più forte del silenzio della notte.
Per tutte le volte
che la tua mano
non riusciva a sfiorare il mio seno
ho sfiorato il tuo viso
con delicata brezza di settembre
Per tutte le volte
che non riesci ad andartene
allontano i miei passi
trattenendo il respiro
per non trattenerti in me
Per tutte le volte
che non riesci a tornare
avvicino il mio viso
al tuo riflesso
sul vetro del tempo.

Looking for Goodbye

For all those times
you couldn't say
"ti amo,"
I've said it for you
stronger than midnight stillness.
For all those times
your hand couldn't
graze my breast,
I've touched your face
with the delicate breeze of September.
For all those times
you don't go away,
I scurry away,
hold my breath
so as not to hold you within me.
For all those times
you can't return,
I put my face
on your reflection
in the pane of time.

Essere e non essere donna

Icona asessuata
scritta all'alba
segnata dal sole nascente
appesa ancora giovane.
Nei suoi colori freschi intuisco
il passare dal tempio dei sensi
al tabernacolo chiuso e freddo
di una immagine
Cola sangue fra tempere secche:
non è una santa è solo viva

To Be and Not to Be a Woman

Asexual icon
sketched at dawn,
marked from the sun's birth,
suspended still in youth
in whose flesh, in its color, I intuit
from the temple of senses a passage
to the locked and cold tabernacle
of one image
dripping blood along dried paint:
no saint, only alive.

Niente più lacrime

Non piangere amore
mentre guardi la pioggia
che lava la paura
rifuggi pensieri
cancella un futuro incerto
Non piangere più
raccogli lacrime in mani
diafane
e fanne dono a questa vita

No More Tears

No teary love.
While you watch rain
wash over fear
and refuse to think,
it shuts out a debatable future.
No more weeping—
catch handfuls
of diaphanous tears
and make of them
a gift to this life.

Normalità

Si avvicina sinuosa
la normalità, si insinua
fra un pensiero e l'altro
riordinando in archivio
gli amori del venerdì,
e quelli del sabato;
lunedì l'agenda svuota
l'alcool della domenica
e nei giorni appresso
la vita seguita a masticare
l'amaro tabacco sputato
dal classificatore metallico

Normal

Writhing, it approaches—
ordinary life slipped
between thoughts
while I'm refiling the archives.
Friday's loves,
and Saturday's;
Monday's agenda drinks up
Sunday's wine
and the days to come;
life will chew up bitter tobacco,
the juice spat
at that metal filing cabinet.

Anfetamine

Dolci, piccole, bianche
diafane creature
che esplodono nei neuroni
in una attività rutilante
E nel mondo che volteggia
spasmi di memoria
abbandonano il corpo
svuotano l'anima
In scalare a poco a poco
sembrano immobili gli altri
e il cervello si sbriciola
come foglia secca d'autunno

Amphetamine

Sweet little white
diaphanous creatures
that explode inside the neurons,
that sparkle.
And in the world that twirls,
memorable spasms
abandon the body,
drain the soul dry.
Climbing back even a little
is to see others stand still,
the brain crumble
like a leaf withered in autumn.

Assenza del dolore

Rinuncio ai pensieri
di rinuncia cambiando
il mio lessico in rivincita.
Il male trasforma gli occhi
che ora guardano più giù
oltre il buio della notte
oltre il mare della disperazione
Tralascio note che illuminano
vite altrui, ognuno
dovrà ora imparare da sè
il limite inesistente
che ci fa credere felicità
l'assenza del dolore

Absence of Pain

I renounce renouncing
and edit my lexicon with a vengeance.
Evil transforms eyes
now turned down low
beyond night's dark
or sea's despair.
I omit notes that could illuminate
lives of others; each of us
will now have to learn from the self
the fabricated boundaries
that make us believe happiness merely
the absence of pain.

Nuvole

Si sussurrano i segreti
alla propria anima
e nel suo continuo svanire
nel suo continuo smarrirsi
i segreti stessi
si fanno nuvole
e le nuvole
rendono il cielo meno solo

Clouds

whisper secrets
to the original soul
and in continuing evaporation,
continued self-dissolution,
the same secrets
become clouds—and the clouds
make heaven less empty.

Sagra

Sagra di tette e culi
in esposizione
ma non sono in vendita!
Gli anni a poco sono serviti,
poche menti brillano
solo per denaro:
scaltre, avide, in cerca di lusso.
Solo questo mi è dato vedere:
triste mestizia
persa su ricchi c/c
di una ricchezza incolore
svuotata ma sempre padrona,
forse unica padrona
Non sembra possibile
vi siano pensieri e sentimenti
non sembra possibile
vi sia un luogo di magia
Taglio col machete liane e rovi
ma non mi lasciano pace
quei vuoti suoni,
miagolii, muggiti, pigolii
di sagra lontana
che a loro sembra felicità,
sembra godimento
e mi chiedo
che cosa significhi "godere"

Feast

Feast of ass and nipple
on display
but not for sale!
The years have had no effect;
small minds glitter
only for money:
cunning, greed, in search of luxury.
I've been given only this to see:
sad melancholy
lost on rich bank accounts
of a pallid treasure,
a mistress forever draining away—
the one and only Mistress Doubt.
It's impossible
to think and to feel anything,
impossible
to stay in that magic land.
I cut blackberry vines with a machete
but they give me no peace,
those meaningless noises:
mewing, lowing, chirping
from the faraway feast
that looks like happiness,
looks like enjoyment,
and I ask
what 's the meaning
of "pleasure."

La morte dell'Avvocato

Una bandiera rossa
legge del contrappasso
nella morte di un vecchio
Ad ogni ruga un solco sanguinante
di strada furente
Al suo respiro un paese
prostrava in ginocchio adorante
Ora sul catafalco nero
giace e la sua morte
è un gioco in borsa
con azioni al rialzo

The Death of *L'Avvocato*

(Giovanni Agnelli, an industrialist and principal shareholder of Fiat)

A red banner
reads retaliation
in an old man's death.
At each wrinkle a bleeding furrow
of street fury.
At his breath a country prostrate,
adoring, on its knees.
Now on the black stage
he lies in state and his death
is a dice roll on the stock exchange,
prices going up.

Planisfero

Una mappa celeste,
la tua schiena.
Ad uno ad uno
bacio dolci nei
sulla pelle bianca
ad uno ad uno
li accarezzo
accarezzando
ogni stella nel cielo.

Planisphere

A celestial map,
your shoulders.
One by one
I kiss sweet moles
on white skin,
one by one
caress them,
caressing
every heavenly star.

Educazione sentimentale (I)

Insegnerete poi amore
e tenerezza quando
vermi ermafroditi
divoreranno le viscere
consumando ciò che fu vivo
Inseguirete tentativi
di scrivere lettere e poesie
d'amore quando l'essere desiderato
preda dei parassiti
non potrà più leggerle

A Sentimental Education (I)

You shall teach love then
and tenderness when
hermaphroditic worms
shall devour the entrails
consuming what was alive.
You'll pursue, trying
to write love letters and poems
of love, though the one you yearn for,
prey of parasites,
can't read them anymore.

Il mio corpo in te

In una goccia ambrata
trasformo il mio corpo,
per entrare in te
delicatamente,
senza disturbare
scivolare veloce
per trovare casa
disperdendomi in te
e non fare più ritorno

My Body In You

I transform my body
into a drop of amber,
the better to enter yours
delicately, not to disturb,
and quickly slip
into my newly discovered home,
scattering inside you,
never more to return.

Amori provvisori

Amori provvisori:
supplenze settimanali
non rimettono in pari
allievi disattenti
Amori transitori
stazionano su binari morti
trascinando in polvere
gli ultimi sentimenti della notte
Amori emarginati
vergognosi guardano
altrove
in falsi ricordi vuoti

Provisional Loves

Provisional
weekly stand-ins
not graded equally,
inattentive students.
Loves in transit
parked beneath unused railroad tracks
dragging in their dust
the utmost feelings of night.
Outcast loves,
shameful, they look elsewhere,
as phony as meaningless
souvenirs.

Occhiali

Rimarrà la mia penna
sotto gli occhiali
nel riposo eterno
tutto verrà gettato
dei miei diari
un solo mucchio
di cenere,
dei miei sogni nessuno
se n'era accorto
e i desideri sono passati
nel filtro di
chi voleva vedere
senza i miei occhiali

Eyeglasses

My pen will stay
under the eyeglasses
in eternal rest.
All of my journals will be tossed
onto a single heap of ash.
No one had noticed my dreams
and desires gone,
filtered through one
who wanted to see
without my glasses

Educazione sentimentale (II)

Provate ora a educare
il vostro cuore e
il pensiero nell'usare parole
che mente umana intenda.
Il tempo della cenere
è vicino e la corruttibilità
della carne pretende
un segno e non
pallida arroganza
di una vita spesa
nell'attesa dell'altrui
comprensione

A Sentimental Education (II)

Now try to educate
your heart & mind
to use words
intentionally human.
The time of ash
is upon us and the corruptibility
of the flesh wants
a sign and not
pallid arrogance
of a life spent
in the shade of others
awaiting comprehension.

Klondike

Paese dell'oro
di miseria
di riscatto
terra di pepite
e palpiti
nella corsa sfrenata
verso materia inorganica
falsamente stabile
falsamente fedele

Klondike

Gold country
of misery,
of redemption,
land of nuggets
and heart throbs
running wild
toward inorganic matter,
falsely stable,
falsely faithful.

Nuovi fratelli

La tua pelle
ti distingue
ti distingue la bandana
sulla fronte
ed i tuoi fianchi
ritmano musiche tribali
Fratello fra fratelli
simili
sensualità nella mano
aperta
e calore nel timore
d'essere respinto

New Brothers

Your skin
distinguishes you,
the bandana on your forehead
distinguishes you,
and your hips
keep the beat
of tribal music.
Brother among brothers
alike,
sensuality of the open hand
and flushed in fear
of being rejected.

In te

S'increspa la tua pelle
con un dito
sfiorando queste onde
che vanno e vengono.
Assopita in te
rannicchiata nel tuo odore
avvolta nel fondo del tuo piacere,
temo il tempo
che ci separa

In You

Your skin twitches
under a fingertip
surfing these waves
that come and go.
Dormant inside you,
tucked within your scent,
shrouded in pleasure,
ticks the hour I fear
that will separate us.

Rinascita

Occhi chiusi
in una cecità apparente
momentanea/paradosso
la musica fluttua
dai piedi scalzi
percorre ogni vena
fino al cuore
e urla dentro
la vita che è pronta
a morire per far
nascere nuove idee
e spezzare vecchie catene

Rebirth

Eyes shut
as if snow-blind,
a momentary paradox,
the flautist's tunes
from bare feet course
upward to every vein
targeting the heart.
Inner life screams
that it's ready
to die for new ideas,
born to snap old chains.

Sugli occhi un bacio

Sugli occhi un bacio
è la colazione del mattino:
e labbra socchiuse
come finestre schiuse
Mi cibo di luce
che trafigge la polvere
tuffando l'amore
in una tazza di tè.

A Kiss on the Eyelids

A kiss on the eyelids
is morning breakfast
and lips half-closed
like windows half-open.
I feed on light
as it traffics the dust,
plunging love
in a cup of tea.

Tributo d’amore

Già pagato il mio tributo all’amore.
Ho amato e amo
nessuno potrà occupare
spazio e tempo.
Ho amato e amo
fino a colmare voragini
di assenza e indifferenza.
Ho amato il passato,
amo l’oggi che non si arrende,
e nel domani il mio amore
sarà un nastro di seta blu
che unisce il tempo

Tax on Love

My tax on love already paid,
I loved and I love
so no one else will fill
the time-space continuum.
I have loved and I love
until I've chasms
of absence and indifference
full to the brim.
I've loved the past,
I love the moment that doesn't surrender,
and tomorrow my love
will be a blue silk ribbon
wrapped about time.

In ogni luogo

Ovunque andrò ti porterò con me
tu parte di me
come foglia dell'albero più tenace
in ogni luogo vivrò per te
Perchè non so per che cos'altro vivere
aspetterò la tua mano
delicata a sfiorare la mia fronte
aspetterò per i tuoi occhi
e per le tue labbra
Ovunque andrò sarà attesa
ma senza solitudine.

Everywhere

Wherever I go I shall take you with me,
you, a part of me
like the leaf of a tree, more tenacious.
Everywhere I will live for you.
I don't know why I should live for any other.
I'll await your hand's
delicate brush of my brow
I'll await your eyes and lips.
Wherever I go I'll keep waiting
but without loneliness.

Passione e vecchiaia

Vecchiaia mi prenderà
prima o poi
e guarderò l'amore con
occhi irretiti dalle rughe
intreccerò poesie
con i fili grigi dei
miei capelli
e accarezzerò il tuo viso
celando la passione
fra le mani che
altri vorrebbero fraterne.

Passion & Aging

Old age will get me
sooner or later
and I'll watch love
with eyes snared in trap lines.
I'll weave poems
with the gray strands of
my hair
and caress your face,
concealing passion
in hands that
others might see as fraternal.

Vestita di vento

Notte di silenzi assordanti
Vestita di vento
E solitudine
Mi sento foglia
Senza sorelle

Dressed on Wind

Nights of deafening silence
dressed in wind
and loneliness:
I'm a leaf
without sisters.

Esseri senza mondo

Ero povera
in un mondo di ricchi
e pazza
in un mondo di savi
annusavo la vita
senza assaggiarla
e la vita del mondo
non era la mia
Ero viva
nel cimitero del mondo
e amavo
nel cimitero del cuore.
Assaggio, ora, la vita a piccoli morsi:
la mia vita che non è del mondo.

To Be Without a World

I was poor
in a world of the rich,
crazed
in a world of the wise.
I sniffed at life
without tasting
and worldly life
wasn't mine.
I lived
in the world's graveyard
and I loved
in the graveyard of the heart
tasting, now, life in nibbling bites:
my life that's not of this world.

Lucia Gazzino was born in Udine (Friuli, Italy) in 1959 and has been a poet since she was a teenager. A teacher of creative writing, she translates history and poetry, and writes both in Italian and in Friulian (her mother tongue). In 2005, Marimbo Press published *The New Youth*, her translation of a selection of Friulian poems by Pier Paolo Pasolini, and in 2010 she was one of the ten translators of *In Danger: a Pasolini Anthology*, published by City Lights Books. She also translated *The Kid's Way*, an anthology of Tibetan poems. Her poems have appeared in various anthologies of Italian poetry and have been translated into German, English, Welsh, and Slovenian. Her books include *Fiori di Papiro*, *La cjase des Cjartis*, *Alter Mundus* and *Babel oms, feminis e cantonîrs*. Her poetic DVD is called *Viaggiatori senza Valigia*. She lives in the Friulian countryside.

Translator's Note
I studied Italian with an Irish priest, French with a Spaniard who knew no English, and Latin and Greek with a Czech. The Bronx-born polyglot, Jack Hirschman, Poet Laureate Emeritus of San Francisco, gave me *Alter Mundus*, Italian poems of Friulan poet, Lucia Gazzino. Her choice in favor of the more durable Latin title rages with Pasolini's *Gospel according to Saint Matthew*—"the poor will always be with you"—and resists complacent acceptance of that fact. I am grateful for assistance and editing to Lucia Gazzino, Jack Hirschman, and Alipio Terenzi.

Michael Daley has translated *Horace: Eleven Odes* (Brooding Heron). He is the author of *Way Out There: Lyrical Essays* (Pleasure Boat Studio), several chapbooks, and three volumes of poetry: *The Straits* (Empty Bowl), *To Curve* (Word), and *Moonlight in the Redemptive Forest* (Pleasure Boat Studio).

Poetry Books from *Pleasure Boat Studio: A Literary Press*

Listed chronologically by release date. *Note:* **Empty Bowl Press** is a Division of Pleasure Boat Studio.

The Every Day ~ Sarah Plimpton ~ $15.95
A Taste ~ Morty Schiff ~ $15.95
Hanoi Rhapsodies ~ Scott Ezell ~ $10 ~ **an empty bowl book**
Dark Square ~ Peter Marcus ~ $14.95
Notes from Disappearing Lake ~ Robert Sund ~ $15
Taos Mountain ~ Paintings and poetry ~ Robert Sund ~ $45 (hardback only)
P'u Ming's Oxherding Pictures & Verses ~ trans. from Chinese by Red Pine ~ $15 ~ **an empty bowl book**
Swimming the Colorado ~ Denise Banker ~ $16 ~ **an empty bowl book**
A Path to the Sea ~ Liliana Ursu, trans. from Romanian by Adam J. Sorkin and Tess Gallagher ~ $15.95
Songs from a Yahi Bow: Poems about Ishi ~ Yusef Komanyakaa, Mike O'Connor, Scott Ezell ~ $13.95
Beautiful Passing Lives ~ Edward Harkness ~ $15
Immortality ~ Mike O'Connor ~ $16
Painting Brooklyn ~ Paintings by Nina Talbot, Poetry by Esther Cohen ~ $20
Ghost Farm ~ Pamela Stewart ~ $13
Unknown Places ~ Peter Kantor, trans. from Hungarian by Michael Blumenthal ~ $14
Moonlight in the Redemptive Forest ~ Michael Daley ~ includes a CD ~ $16
Lessons Learned ~ Finn Wilcox ~ $10 ~ **an empty bowl book**
Jew's Harp ~ Walter Hess ~ $14
The Light on Our Faces ~ Lee Whitman-Raymond ~ $13
Petroglyph Americana ~ Scott Ezell ~ $15 ~ **an empty bowl book**
God Is a Tree, and Other Middle-Age Prayers ~ Esther Cohen ~ $10
Home & Away: The Old Town Poems ~ Kevin Miller ~ $15
Old Tale Road ~ Andrew Schelling ~ $15 ~ **an empty bowl book**
Working the Woods, Working the Sea ~ Eds. Finn Wilcox, Jerry Gorsline ~ $22 ~ **an empty bowl book**
The Blossoms Are Ghosts at the Wedding ~ Tom Jay ~ with essays ~ $15 ~ **an empty bowl book**
Against Romance ~ Michael Blumenthal ~ $14
Days We Would Rather Know ~ Michael Blumenthal ~ $14
Craving Water ~ Mary Lou Sanelli ~ $15
When the Tiger Weeps ~ Mike O'Connor ~ with prose ~ 15
Concentricity ~ Sheila E. Murphy ~ $13.95
The Immigrant's Table ~ Mary Lou Sanelli ~ with recipes ~ $14
Women in the Garden ~ Mary Lou Sanelli ~ $14
Saying the Necessary ~ Edward Harkness ~ $14
Nature Lovers ~ Charles Potts ~ $10
The Politics of My Heart ~ William Slaughter ~ $13
The Rape Poems ~ Frances Driscoll ~ $13

Our Chapbook Series:

No. 1: ***The Handful of Seeds: Three and a Half Essays*** ~ Andrew Schelling ~ $7 ~ nonfiction
No. 2: ***Original Sin*** ~ Michael Daley ~ $8
No. 3: ***Too Small to Hold You*** ~ Kate Reavey ~ $8
No. 4: ***The Light on Our Faces*—re-issued in non-chapbook (see previous list)**
No. 5: ***Eye*** ~ William Bridges ~ $8
No. 6: ***Selected* New Poems *of Rainer Maria Rilke*** ~ trans. fm German by Alice Derry ~ $10
No. 7: ***Through High Still Air: A Season at Sourdough Mountain*** ~ Tim McNulty ~ $9 ~ with prose
No. 8: ***Sight Progress*** ~ Zhang Er, trans. fm Chinese by Rachel Levitsky ~ $9 ~ prosepoems
No. 9: ***The Perfect Hour*** ~ Blas Falconer ~ $9
No. 10: ***Fervor*** ~ Zaedryn Meade ~ $10
No. 11: ***Some Ducks*** ~ Tim McNulty ~ $10
No. 12: ***Late August*** ~ Barbara Brackney ~ $10
No. 13: ***The Right to Live Poetically*** ~ Emily Haines ~ $9

From other publishers (in limited editions):

Desire ~ Jody Aliesan ~ $14 ~ **an empty bowl book**
Dreams of the Hand ~ Susan Goldwitz ~ $14 ~ **an empty bowl book**
The Basin: Poems from a Chinese Province ~ Mike O'Connor ~ $10/$20 ~ **an empty bowl book** (paper/hardbound)
The Straits ~ Michael Daley ~ $10 ~ **an empty bowl book**
In Our Hearts and Minds: The Northwest and Central America ~ Ed. Michael Daley ~ $12 ~ with prose ~ **an empty bowl book**
The Rainshadow ~ Mike O'Connor ~ $16 ~ **an empty bowl book**
Untold Stories ~ William Slaughter ~ $10/$20 ~ **an empty bowl book** (paper/hardbound)
In Blue Mountain Dusk ~ Tim McNulty ~ $12.95 ~ **an empty bowl book**
China Basin ~ Clemens Starck ~ $13.95 ~ a Story Line Press book
Journeyman's Wages ~ Clemens Starck ~ $10.95 ~ a Story Line Press book

Orders: Pleasure Boat Studio books are available by order from your bookstore, directly from our website, or through the following:
SPD (Small Press Distribution) Tel. 800-869-7553, Fax 510-524-0852
Partners/West Tel. 425-227-8486, Fax 425-204-2448
Baker & Taylor Tel. 800-775-1100, Fax 800-775-7480
Ingram Tel. 615-793-5000, Fax 615-287-5429
Amazon.com or **Barnesandnoble.com**

Pleasure Boat Studio: A Literary Press
201 West 89th Street
New York, NY 10024
Tel./Fax: 888-810-5308
www.pleasureboatstudio.com / pleasboat@nyc.rr.com